KRUPP AT WAR

The Legendary Krupp Protze & Other Vehicles

Reinhard Frank

At left:
A group of Krupp L 2 H 143 trucks as personnel carriers (Kfz.70) proves its off-road capability in Russia. The white "G" indicates Panzer Group 2 (Guderian). Note the two-line license plates on the front bumper. Unfortunately, the division emblem on the BMW R 12 motorcycle cannot be read clearly.

SCHIFFER MILITARY HISTORY
West Chester, PA

Cover Artwork by Steve Ferguson, Colorado Springs, CO
Additional Research by Russell Mueller

KRUPP KRAFTWAGEN "BOXER"

On the plains of the Ukraine beneath a red morning sky, a Luftwaffe "Boxer" flak crew swings into action as their spotter calls out aircraft approaching from the east. The truck's standard RLM dark grey is augmented by white trim on the front fenders and a draped flag over the forward rack for quick identification by friendly aircrews, and paradoxically covered with branches to obscure its square profile from the enemy.

Mounting a single 20mm Flak 30 gun, the Boxers were pressed into service to cover the rapidly advancing Luftwaffe units that swept into Russia as part of the Wehrmacht's massive Operation "Barbarossa" in the summer of 1941. Unarmored and underpowered, more powerful vehicles with heavier armament soon replaced the Boxer. By 1942, Krupp's mass produced Kraftrwagen was still in use, but its flak battery career had long since been curtailed.

Bibliography

D 600 "Anhaltswerte über Kfz.u.Gerät", 1940
D 669/9 "Lastkraftwagen 1 1/2 t Krupp Typ L 2 H 143, Gerätebeschreibung u. Bedienungsanweisung zum Fahrgestell", 1941
D 669/303 "Lastkraftwagen 1 1/2 t Krupp Typ L 2 H 143, Instandsetzungsanleitung", 1943
L.Dv. 650 "vorläufiger Beladeplan für Flak-Messtrupp KW. I und II", 1934
L.Dv. 654/1 (H.Dv.180) "Beladeplan für eine Flakbatterie zu 12 Geschützen 20mm Flak 30 (mot.Z), 1939
Kruppsche Monatshefte
Technical information supplied by Krupp
Fried. Krupp GmbH — Historical Archives
Deutschen Museum, Munich
Podzun-Pallas Verlag Archives

Special thanks to Gertrud, Stefan and Daniel, my friends and assistants Robert Emmert, Heinz Friedrich, Horst Scheibert, Leo Schmitt and Peter Taghon.

Reinhard Frank, Schmidgern 20, 8031 Gilching.

Translated from the German by Edward Force.

Printed in the United States of America.
ISBN: 0-88740-399-9

This title was originally published under the title,
Krupp-Kraftwagen im Kriege,
by Podzun-Pallas Verlag, Friedberg.

We are interested in hearing from authors with book ideas on related topics. We are also looking for good photographs in the military history area. We will copy your photos and credit you should your materials be used in a future Schiffer project.

Published by Schiffer Publishing, Ltd.
1469 Morstein Road
West Chester, Pennsylvania 19380
Please write for a free catalog.
This book may be purchased from the publisher.
Please include $2.95 postage.
Try your bookstore first.

Foreword

The legendary Krupp name, can be traced back to 1587 in Essen. The steel tradition of the house of Krupp began in 1800 with the purchase of the "Good Hope" mill, and later a cast-steel factory was founded in 1811. The most important invention in 1853 was the seamless railroad-wheel, which became the firm's emblem, as three joined rings, in 1875. Despite frequent financial crises, the firm expanded steadily. Production during World War I was converted almost exclusively to armaments, especially guns and ammunition. After the Treaty of Versailles, Krupp was forced to change to the production of other products (special steels, locomotives, farm machinery, public works vehicles, engines (for trucks), etc.

The "Truck Factory Department" went into business in 1919. The first model made in large numbers was the "Five-ton with 75 HP 4-cylinder Otto Engine" of 1920. In 1924 there came 1.5-, 2.5- and 3-ton high-speed trucks, in 1925 a modified 5-ton type. The first buses with low-frame chassis appeared in 1928. Until World War II, Krupp offered a large assortment of trucks with varying frame heights (H, M, N), engines (gasoline, Diesel, woodgas) and loads (1.5, 2, 2.5, 3, 3.5, 4, 5, 5.5, 6.5 tons).

The factory did pioneering work in engine construction through the development of high-performance truck carburetors and Diesel engines with air-cooling.

There were 50-, 55-, 60- and 80-HP Diesel engines (their own developments), 60-, 90- and 125-HP Diesel engines (under license from Junkers), 60-, 65-, 75-, 110- and 150-HP carburetor engines, and 65-HP woodgas engines.

In 1937 the number of finished vehicles added up to 4300, made by a work force of 2685 employees. In 1939, official requirements limited production of civilian vehicles to the 3-ton and 6.5-ton trucks. In 1940 Krupp was obligated to build 12-ton heavy towing tractors (Sd.Kfz.8) under license. In 1941 only the L 2 H 143, single engines and the Sd.Kfz.8 were produced. In 1942 production of the Protzkraftwagen, of which 200 per month were built in the end, was halted. In that year 3403 employees were on the payroll.

The first heavy air raids on Essen and the factory took place in March, 1943. By war's end, 70% of the firm's facilities had been destroyed or damaged. Between 1946 and 1952, 75% of the remaining facilities were dismantled or scrapped. The business was then broken up. The "Kraftwagenfabrik" became the "Südwerke" firm of Kulmbach. Their best-known truck was the "Titan", with a 210-HP 6-cylinder Diesel engine.

The type designations of Krupp trucks are confusing at first glance, but contain much information. For example, "LD 2 H 142" means:

L = Lastwagen (truck)
D = Diesel engine
2 = load capacity in tons
H = light frame
1 = first modification
4 = 4-cylinder
2 = two-axle

ABBREVIATIONS:

l. = light
m. = medium
s. = heavy
gp. = armored
gl. = off-road capable
(o) = standard
Kfz. = motor vehicle
Kw. = vehicle
Lkw. = truck
Pz.Kpfw. = armored military vehicle
Sd.Ah. = special trailer
Sd.Kfz. = special motor vehicle

Light Off-Road-Capable 1.5-ton Truck Type L 2 H 43 - L 2 H 143

On the basis of good experience with the L 3 H 63, Krupp set out in 1929 to build a light three-axle (6x4) truck with off-road capability. It came on the market in 1930 as the L 2 H 43. This vehicle had an air-cooled horizontally opposed 4-cylinder gasoline engine, synchronized four-speed gearbox, an additional shift for road or off-road gears, and driven rear wheels suspended on double swing axles.

Several test models were fitted with Diesel engines or support wheels on the front bumper. Series production with a 55-HP carbureted engine was begun in 1932. In 1936 the L 2 H 143 came out with, among other things, a 60-HP engine, a lengthened front bumper and a larger distance between the rear axles.

These robust and modern trucks were used by the Wehrmacht primarily as gun tractors and personnel carriers. Production ended in 1942.

Two trucks were fitted with 70-HP carbureted engines for testing and designated L 2 H 243. One was then equipped with a 70-HP carbureted engine and auxiliary front-wheel drive (6x6), which increased its weight by 350 kg; it was called L 2 H 343. Neither type went into production.

The grandfather of all Krupp army trucks was this 1929 "light off-road truck with air-cooled carbureted or Diesel engine, L 2 H 43 or LD 2 H 43." The engine hood did not yet have the typical angled form, so as to leave room for the bigger (50-HP) Diesel engine. The gasoline engine produced 60 HP.

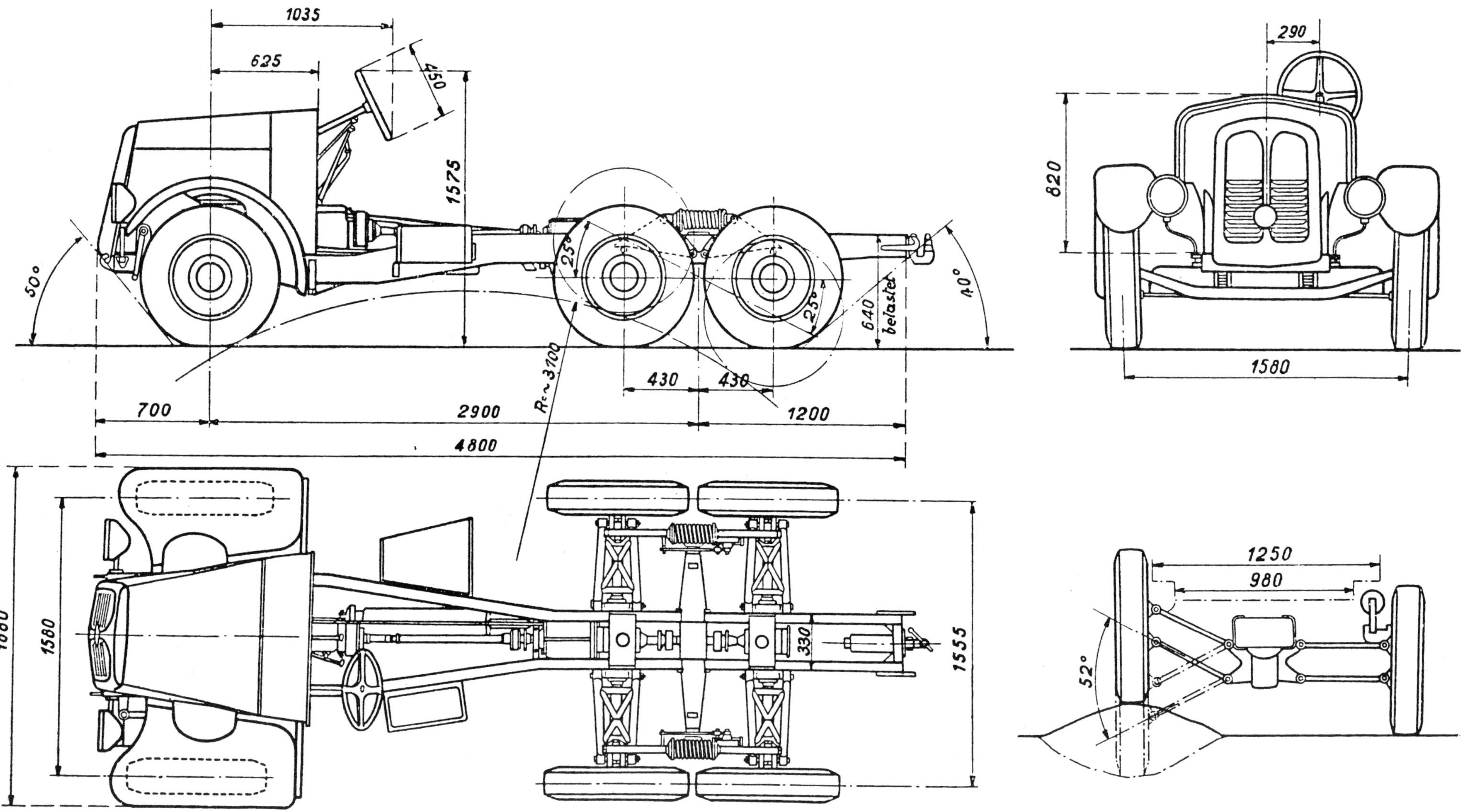

The "Light off-road truck L 2 H 43 or LD 2 H 43" with high engine hood.

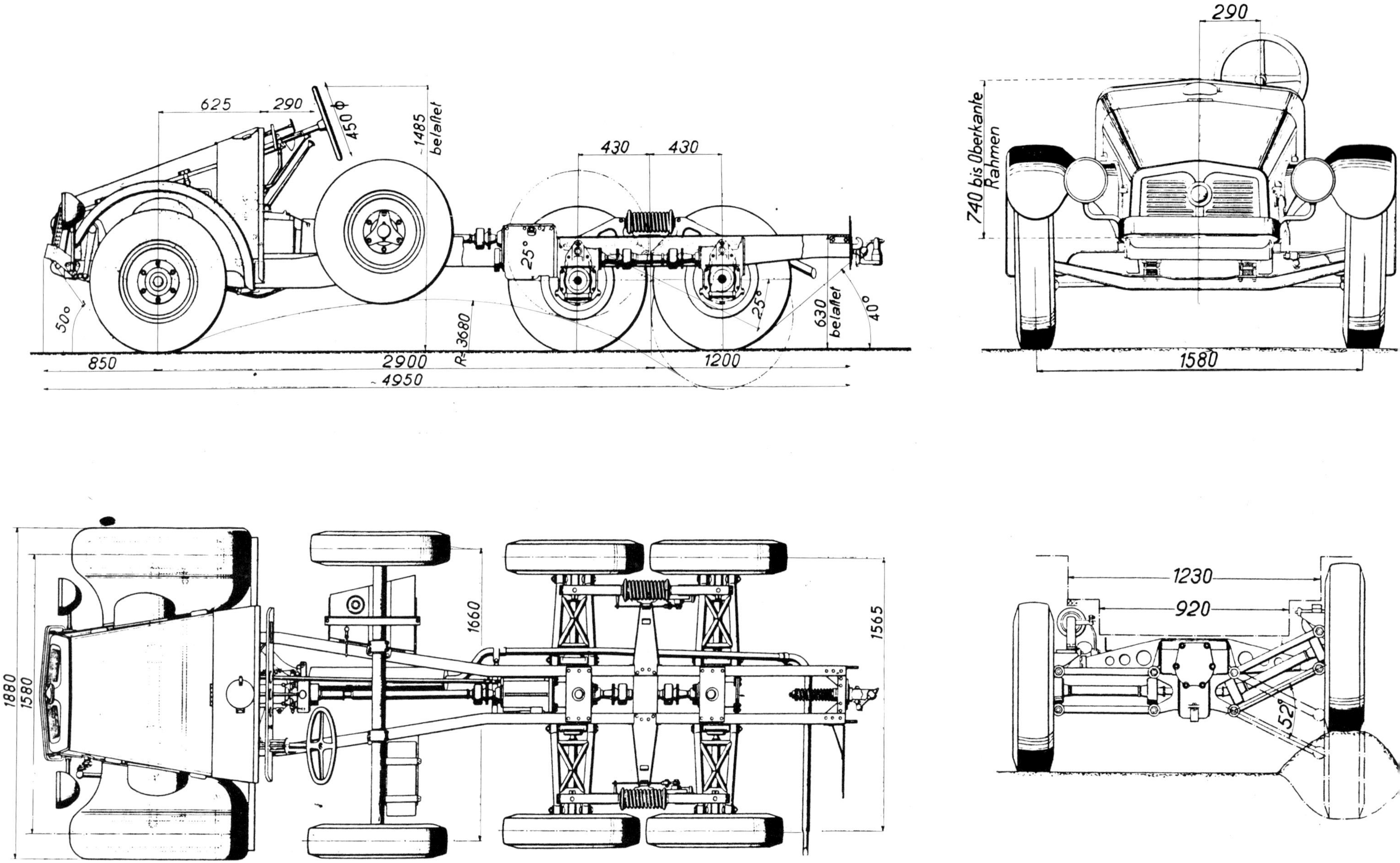

The "Off-road truck L 2 H 43", as it was built from 1932 to 1936 and introduced in the Wehrmacht as "l.gl.Lkw (o)." The successor model L 2 H 143 had longer front bumpers and a distance of 900 mm between rear axles.

The chassis of the L 2 H 143:
1. Axle contact, 2. Rear spring, 3. Accumulator, 4. Stub axle, 5. Steering wheel, 6. Change gears Gb 35 bl, 7. Instrument panel, 8. Reserve fuel tank, 9. Three-way valve, 10. Fuel tank, 11. Auxiliary gearbox GG 35, 12. Middle axle drive, 13. Bumper, 14. Brake line, 15. Trailer hitch, 16. Rear axle drive, 17. Retaining roller, 18. Transverse link, 19. Rear axle shafts, 20. Wheel holder.

Below: The chassis of the L 2 H 143:
1. Instrument panel, 2. Change gears, 3. Steering wheel, 4. Spare wheel, 5. Stub axle, 6. Spare wheel, 7. Driveshaft, 8. Frame, 9. Auxiliary gears, 10. Middle axle drive, 11. Rear spring, 12. Rear axle drive, 13. Trailer hitch.

Left: Engine of the L 2 H 143, Model M 304, 3308 cc, 52 HP at 2500 rpm according to D 669/9, 60 HP according to factory information. I. Fuel valve, 2. Distributor, 3. Filter, 4. Carburetor control rod, 5. Carburetor, 6. Oil-bath air filter, 7. Left intake pipe, 8. Heat cap, 9. Right intake pipe, 10. Fuel mixture warmer, 11. Coil, 12. Upper lid with mixing chamber, 13. Air outlet and oil intake, 14. Radiator shell.

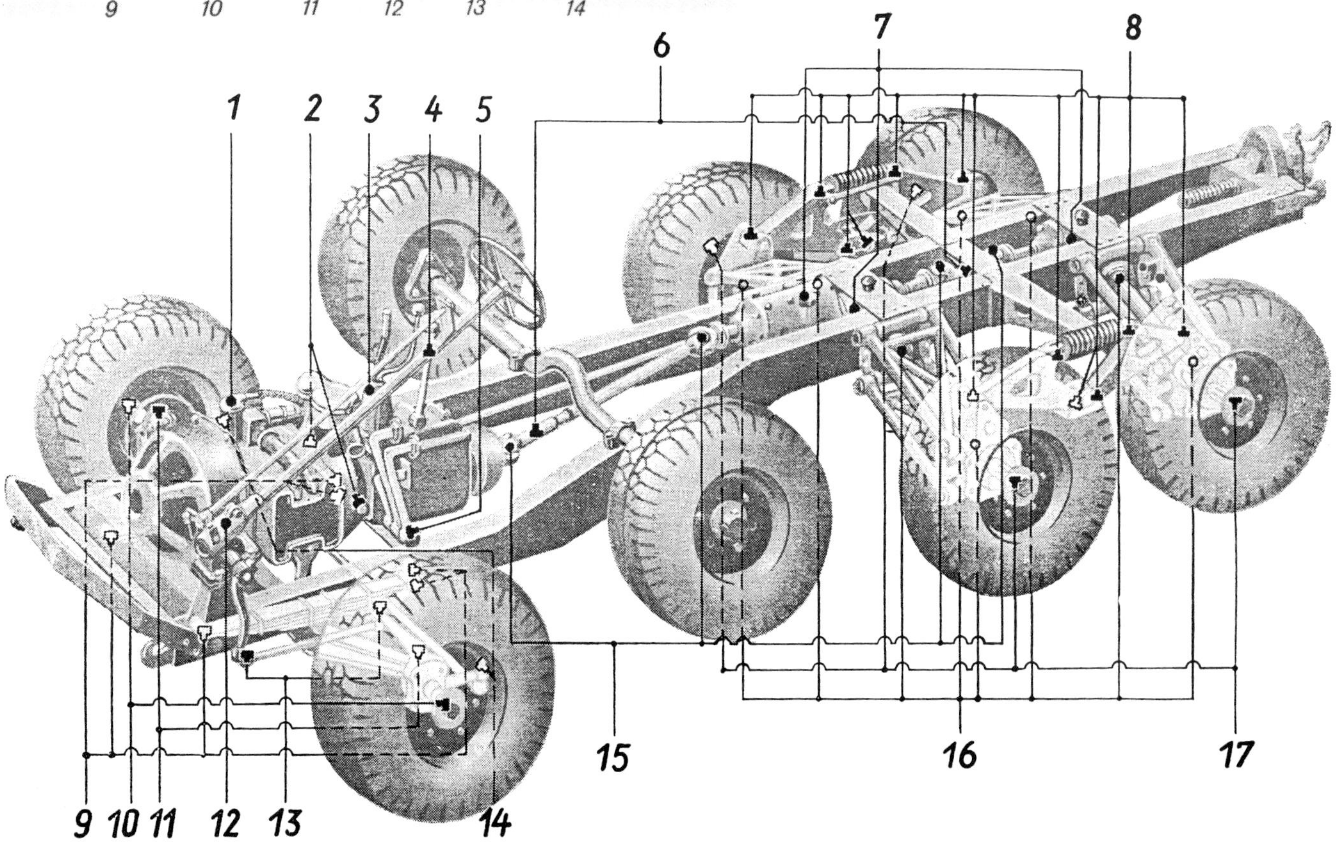

Left: Lubricating diagram of the L 2 H 143; the 34 lubricating nipples were to be provided with lubricant every 3000 to 6000 kilometers. Motor oil had to be changed every 3000 km, gearbox oil every 6000 km.

Left: Krupp L 2 H 143 as a personnel carrier (Kfz.70) with MG 13 machine gun on an anti-aircraft pivot. Crew: one driver and eight men. Note the vehicle's low rear sides.

Lower left: French campaign, 1940: a Krupp L 2 H 143 as personnel carrier (Kfz.70) in MG Battalion 6. The headlights and spotlights are camouflaged.

Below: A Krupp L 2 H 143 as Kfz.70 of the Luftwaffe.

Krupp L 2 H 143 trucks as personnel carriers (Kfz.70) of MG Battalion 6 in Coburg. Note the non-standard technical details of the truck in front: higher cover and spotlight, different attachment of the direction indicators, side wind deflectors, cover snaps and greater distance between windshield and engine hood.

Above: A personnel carrier (Kfz.70) of MG Battalion 6, Coburg. This L 2 H 143 still bears camouflage paint, two-thirds dark gray, one-third dark brown.

Below: A dust-covered L 2 H 143 as a personnel carrier (Kfz.70) of MG Battalion 6, Coburg. Note the MG 34 with aircraft sight, ammunition cases, axe with hook and civilian tail lights, which were customary until the night-marching device was introduced.

Left: Two Krupp L 2 H 143 trucks with different bodies. At left is a "standard" Kfz.70, at right a truck with less space under the windshield, no spare wheel cover, low sides with gaps, thin bridge panels and no storage boxes on the rear fenders.

Right: A personnel carrier (Kfz.70) of the 8th Company of Rifle Regiment 1 at Sennelager in September of 1937.

September 1939: Krupp L 2 H 143 trucks as personnel carriers (Kfz.70) for the 5th company of a motorized infantry unit (probably a rifle battalion) in Poland.

Right: The crew of this personnel carrier (Kfz.70), a Krupp L 2 H 143, waits impatiently for damage to be repaired.

Left: A personnel carrier (Kfz.70) of the motorized riflemen. Although the front bumper is missing, as in some early models, the distance between the rear axles suggests that this may be an L 2 H 143. Note the low sides.

Above: A 1940 advertisement (Ball bearings and roller bearings in Wehrmacht vehicles).

Upper left: This personnel carrier was destroyed and burned out near Amiens in 1940. The crew's fate is unknown. A complete lack of armor made these trucks vulnerable to even light weapons.

Left: The Krupp L 2 H 143 as a light anti-aircraft gun truck. b. Pickaxe, c. Claw hatchet, e. Barrel case for 20mm Flak 30, f. 1 m R 36 range finder.

Krupp L 2 H 143 as light anti-aircraft gun truck (Kfz.81) with 20mm Flak 30 on Special Trailer (Sd.Ah.51). Crew: one driver and six men. A light Flak battery (motorized platoon) consisted of twelve such guns.

Light anti-aircraft truck (Kfz.81): d. Wire cutters, g. Disc wheel with tire for Sd.Ah.51, h. Shoulder rack for Em 1R device, i. Case for linear sight, k. Case for lights, l. Small Device 31 in folding case, m. Towline, n. Flak sight 35, o. Magazine case 30, each with two Mag. 32 or 38, each holding 20 explosive shells, p. Spare parts case for 20mm Flak 30, q. Cleaning case for 20mm K 30, r. Supply case for 20mm Flak 30, s. Guns, t. Magazine case 30 (antitank shells), u. Same as o, v. Machine-gun bullet case, w. Same as v.

Troop parade in Munich on April 20, 1939. Krupp L 2 H 143 as light anti-aircraft gun truck (Kfz.81) with 20mm Flak 30 on Sd.Ah.51. At that time, Flak Regiment 5 and the 1st Flak Unit 75 (ex-II./5) were located in Munich.

Right: Krupp L 2 H 143 as light anti-aircraft truck (Kfz.81) with 20mm Flak 30 on Sd.Ah.51.

Left: "Flak forward!" in Russia. The bows for the cover are left in place. Krupp L 2 H 143 as Kfz.81.

Above: This Krupp L 2 H 143 as Kfz.81 shows its climbing ability in the Bavarian Alps.

Upper left: A Flak unit marches out with their Kfz.81, obviously the whole second (light) unit of a Flak regiment, consisting of the 6th, 7th and 8th batteries. A light battery included twelve 20mm Flak 30 guns, two to four 60 cm spotlights, and was divided into four platoons. (Krupp L 2 H 143).

Left: Krupp L 2 H 143 as light anti-aircraft truck (Kfz.81) advancing in Russia. The 20mm Flak 30 is equipped with a 6 mm, 112 kg shield.

Left: The traverse of this light anti-aircraft (Kfz.81) truck's 20mm Flak 30 gun was limited to the front sector. Note the ammunition cases attached to the sides and the reduced shield.

Lower left: In a number of light anti-aircraft (L 2 H 143, Kfz.81) trucks, the gun was mounted on the rear bed to form a makeshift self-propelled mount. The gun shown here was raised by building up its mount to afford a usable traverse field.

Below: A light anti-aircraft truck (L 2 H 143, Kfz.81) carrying a 20mm Flak 30 gun securing a river crossing. The crew has given themselves a bit of cover by using tent panels.

Above: Krupp L 2 H 143 as light spotlight truck I (Kfz.83). Crew: One driver and four men. In the back is the 8-kilowatt generator with a cable to the 60 cm spotlight. Note the canvas cover on the driver's side. Every light or medium Flak battery had a spotlight echelon with up to four 60 cm spotlights.

Left: Flanders 1940: A light spotlight truck I (Kfz.83) of the "General Göring" regiment, Krupp L 2 H 143. The asymmetrical cylinder cover between the engine hood and fender, the projecting "attachment for starting crank" (usually covered with a sheet-metal cap), and the towed 60 cm anti-aircraft spotlight can be seen here.

Light spotlight truck I (Krupp L 2 H 143, Kfz.83) in Flanders, 1940. The emblem of the "General Göring" regiment is seen clearly.

Right: Krupp L 2 H 143 as light spotlight truck II (Kfz.83). Crew: Driver and four men. These trucks carried the spotlight echelon's equipment and fuel.

Left: Light spotlight truck I (Kfz.83) in Flanders, 1940. The tactical emblem, a triangle, could refer to the third unit, the Flak spotlight unit, which was usually equipped with 150 cm spotlights.

Above: Krupp L 2 H 143 as towing truck (Kfz.69) with 37mm Pak in France, 1940. Here one sees another type of ammunition cases, tall with handles.

Above: This towing truck (Kfz.69) with 37mm Pak gun has low, wide ammunition cases. The rear spare wheel was apparently removed by the Schirmeister. Note the transverse bridge panels, fire extinguisher at right, and Model 16 helmets.

Upper left: Krupp L 2 H 143 as towing truck (Kfz.69). Crew: Driver and five men. This type gave all light off-road Krupp trucks the name of "Krupp-Protze." They were generally used to tow 37mm Pak guns. The crew sat in pairs facing the front or back and could get out either at the front or the back. The body had no sides, but carried four ammunition cases on each side, which were lashed to the fenders with tension wires. There were various types of ammunition cases; here we see the thin, high type. At the back there was sometimes, as here, a rack for two rifles and a spare tire.

Above: Instrument panel and windshield of the Krupp L 2 H 143 as Kfz.69. 1. Socket, 2. Direction indicator, 3. Speedometer, 4. Oil-pressure gauge, 5. Direction indicator switch, 6. Windshield wiper, 7. Fuel valve, 8. Windshield, 9. Attaching screw.

Upper left: Detailed view from D 669/309, August 16, 1943 edition. Note the high winch, lack of spotlights, rifle rack and windshield brace on the engine hood. 1. Wing nut, 2. Driver's seat. (Krupp L 2 H 143 as Kfz.69).

Left: Instead of having a spare wheel mount, this truck had a simple rifle rack and simplified footrest. The sprung trailer hitch with hook and bolt can be seen. The back-up lights have been covered and the brake-light lens is smaller than that of the taillight. (Krupp L 2 H 143 as Kfz.69).

Left: Krupp L 2 H 143 as towing truck (Kfz.69), according to its tactical emblem a vehicle of Panzerjäger Unit 19 (19th Panzer Division). The soldiers are still wearing Model 16 helmets.

Lower left and below: The rare Krupp L 2 H 43 as towing truck (Kfz.69). The direction indicators are attached with flat metal pieces. The wide leather belt of the soldier at left was used to turn and aim the gun. The death's-head emblem on the field caps indicate (former) members of Cavalry Regiment 5. The license plate indicates Military District XI, Hannover, thus this may be a vehicle of Panzerjäger Unit 19. On the left fender is a heart, later the emblem of the 87th Infantry Division.

Above: A towing truck (Kfz.69) from Zone III (Berlin). The top bows are stowed behind the driver's seat and the tire of the spare wheel is missing. The tactical emblem is that of Panzerjäger Unit 23 of the 23rd Infantry Division (Potsdam).

Upper left: A Krupp L 2 H 43 as towing truck (Kfz.69) underway. The crew's means of egress is easy to see.

Left: Sandy Russian roads delayed the off-road towing truck and compelled the crews to push. In the background, the Dretun supply depot is burning (July 1941, 19th P.D.).

Right: "Advance to the Narew near Wizna." The crew of a towing truck (Kfz.69) waits for the tanks to go into action. At right is a Panzer IV tank, Type C, at left rear a Panzer I. (Krupp L 2 H 143)

Left: Amiens 1940; a Krupp L 2 H 143 as towing truck (Kfz.69) with cover in place. The front and spare tires look rather flat! Tactical emblem: 2nd company of a Panzerjäger unit. The obligatory rolls of wire are hung on the windshield frame. These were used to barricade roads quickly, especially against wheeled vehicles.

Upper left: Leningrad area, 1941. Krupp L 2 H 143 as towing truck (Kfz.69) with 75mm light infantry gun 18.(BA)

Upper right: Gray-clad visitors to Paris with a Krupp L 2 H 143 (Kfz.69). Note the simplified footrests, rifle racks and container by the direction indicator.

Left: Action photos of Krupp towing trucks with special bodies are rare. This is a "radio truck (Kfz.61) with chassis of light off-road truck (o)", a Krupp L 2 H 143 of the 19th P.D.

Above: Krupp L 2 H 143 as telephone truck (Kfz.19). Crew: driver and five men. It is not known why this vehicle was not introduced as Kfz.61.

Upper and lower right and below: Krupp L 2 H 143 as radio mast truck (Kfz.68). This truck also existed on uniform Diesel and Magirus chassis. The expensive, manifold development of special vehicle types critically slowed the Wehrmacht's motorized capabilities.

Above: The "group car" developed by Krupp on the L 2 H 143 chassis was not adopted by the Wehrmacht.

Upper left: The construction of small series of three-axle off-road "command cars"seemed to be regarded by the leading vehicle constructors as unavoidable for reasons of prestige. This is a command car on L 2 H 143 chassis. The high engine hood resembles that of the early Krupp Diesel trucks. There were also some vehicles with angled hoods.

Left: No information on this meeting of German officials in Russia is available. At left are two Mercedes-Benz Type G 4 cars, at right a Krupp "command car" on L 2 H 143 chassis.

In 1938 Krupp introduced a well-formed road-going armored car on the L 2 H 143 chassis, but it was not adopted by the Wehrmacht. There is, though, a Russian newsreel that shows such a vehicle, bearing a German cross, in the yard of the Chancellery in Berlin, 1945.

Krupp L 2 H 143 as "s.gl.gp. personnel car (Sd.Kfz.247)", made only in small numbers. At least one such vehicle was still used by the 166th P.D. in 1944.

Below: A Krupp L 2 H 143 with special body for airport service.

Medium Off-Road Truck Type L 3 H 63 - L 3 H 163

In 1928 Krupp introduced its first off-road three-axle (6x4) truck, the L 3 H 63. The vehicle had much the same chassis as the three-ton (1927-28 model), an upright 6-cylinder carbureted engine producing 90 HP, a 4-speed transmission, an auxiliary gearshift for road or off-road speeds, and live rear axles with individual locking differentials. In the middle of the truck, on the right side, was a motor-driven winch with 3-ton towing capability.

In 1936, the engine was upgraded to 110 HP, the gearbox and suspension were strengthened, and the six-wheel hydraulic brakes were replaced by Knorr air-brakes on the rear wheels. The body was unchanged. The clearest identifying marks are two hatches on the engine hood in place of cooling louvers. In the Wehrmacht this vehicle was used with a wide variety of bodies. Production ended in 1938.

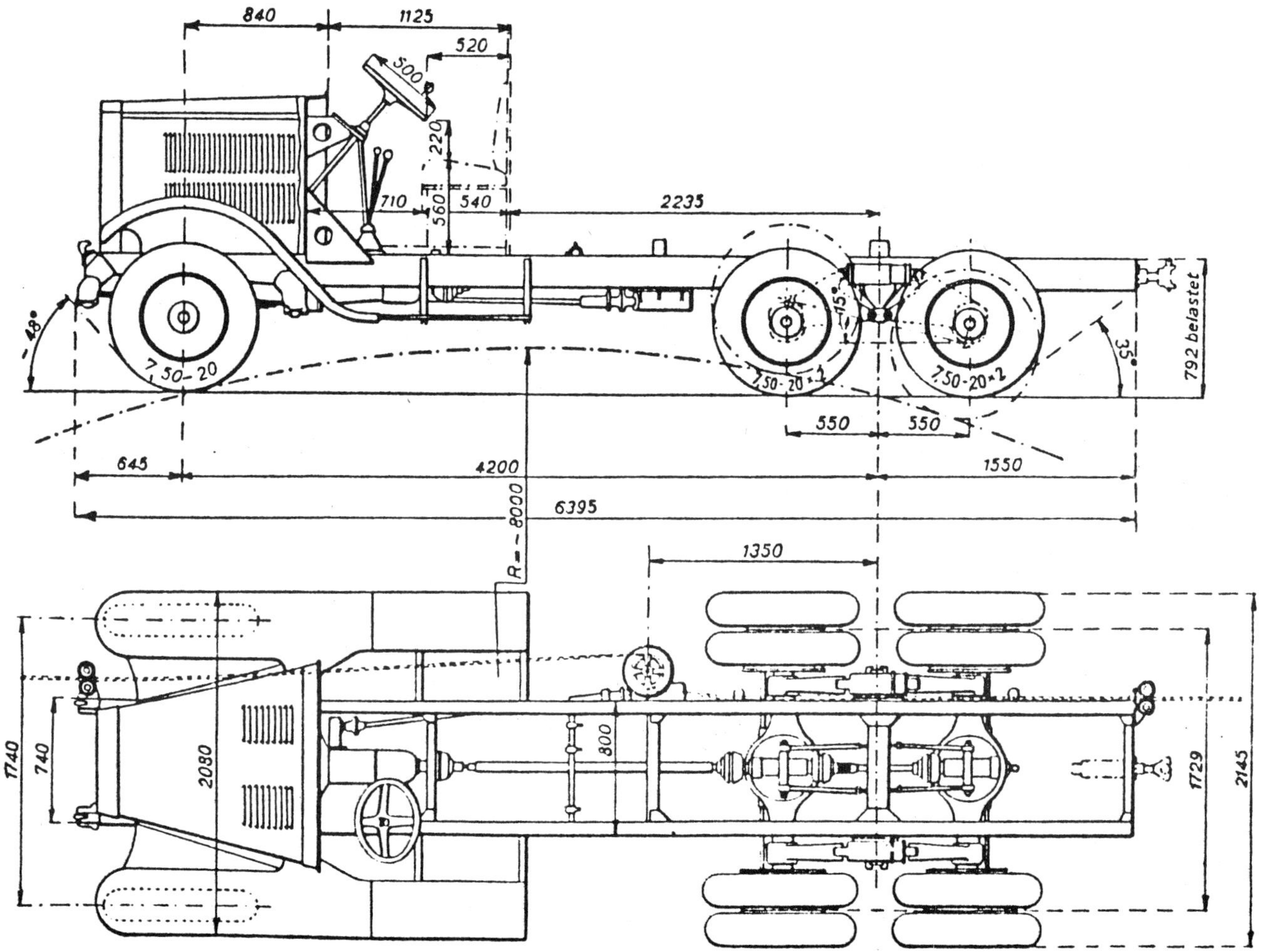

Factory drawing of the Krupp L 3 H 63 chassis.

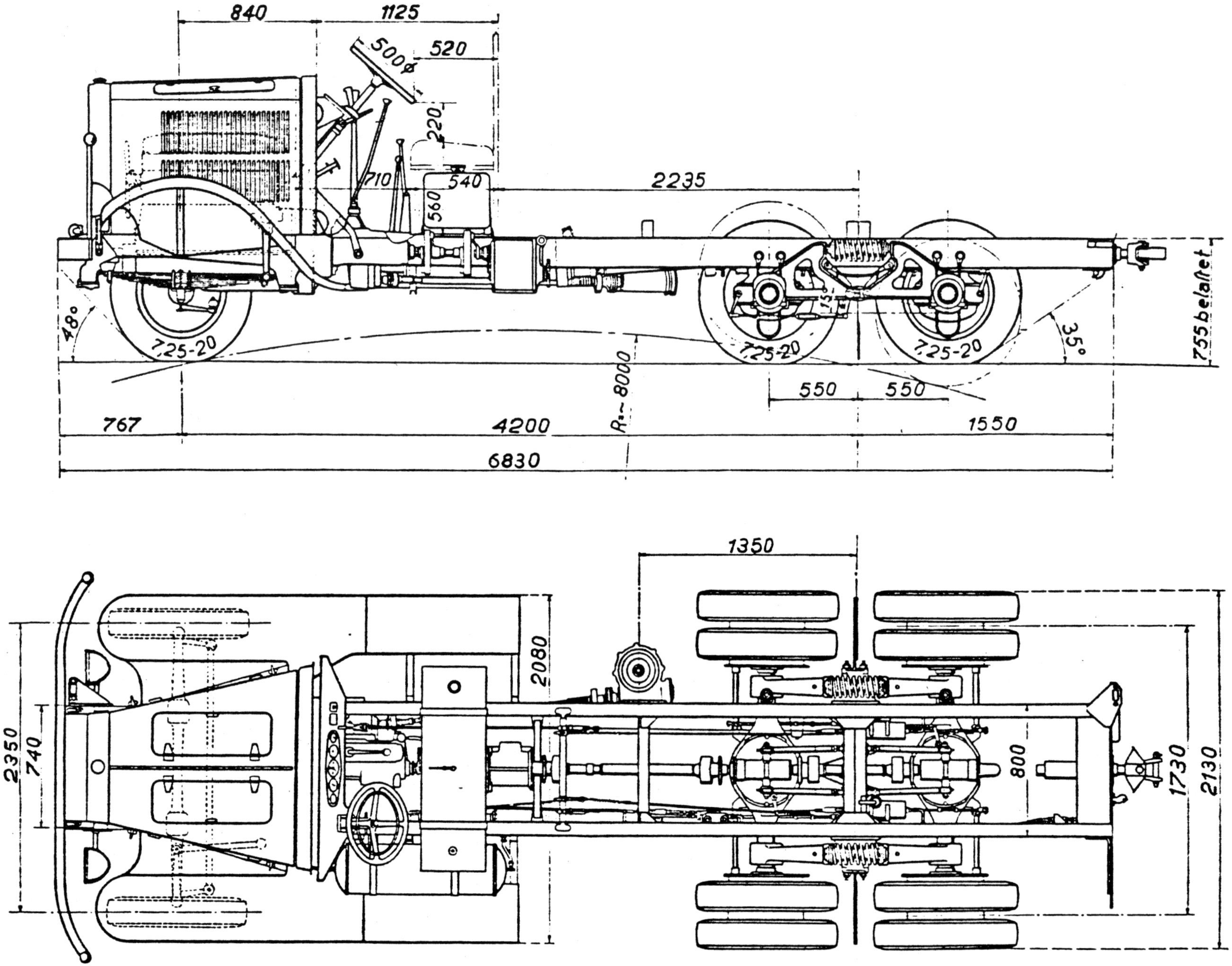

Factory drawing of the Krupp L 3 H 163 chassis. The 2350 mm measurement refers to the bumper; the front track was 1740 mm. This type was also called "L 3 H 63 strengthened" in factory information. In the Wehrmacht it was "m.gl.Lkw.(o)."

Above: Krupp L 3 H 163 as radio listening truck (Kfz.72). This vehicle was also used as a radio, weather and print shop truck.

Upper left: Krupp L 3 H 163 as photography truck (Kfz.354). Crew: Driver and six men.

Left: A Krupp L 3 H 163 at a Russian airfield with I.G. 51. It was used either as Kfz.72 (radio truck) or Kfz.301 (radio mast truck). The column of smoke rising from two points, and the steel helmet of the soldier at right, suggest a successful enemy air attack.

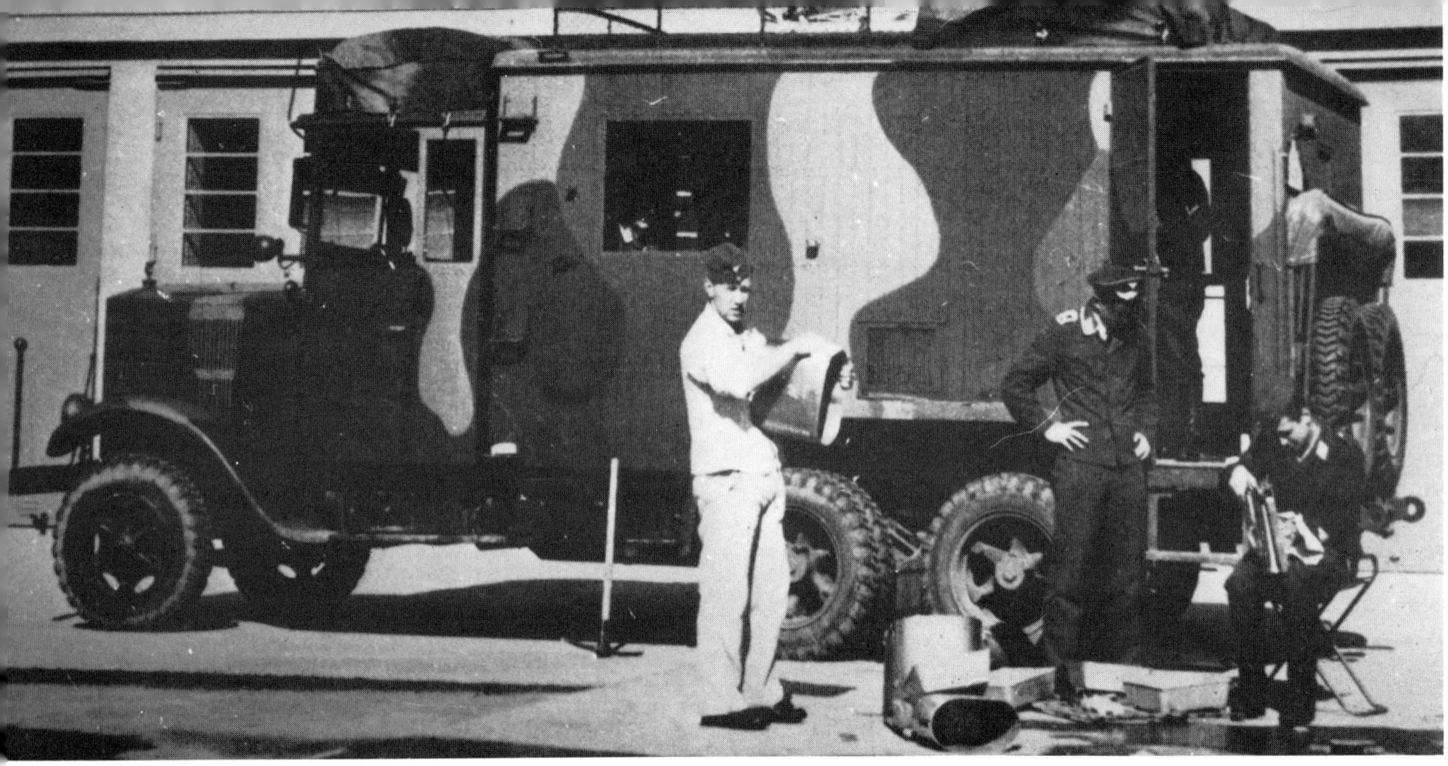

Left: The Krupp L 3 H 163 as a photography truck (Kfz.354) was used by the reconnaissance units of the Luftwaffe. This truck still bears gray-green-brown camouflage paint.

Below: A Krupp L 3 H 163 of Reconnaissance Group 25, most likely a photography truck (Kfz.354), in Russia, winter 1942-43.

Left: Krupp L 3 H 163 medium spotlight trucks with 150 cm spotlights on Sd.Anh.104 trailers, in Hitler's birthday parade in Berlin, 1939. These vehicles had no official number.

Lower left: Krupp L 3 H 163 as field cable trucks; this type also had no number, as it was simply a "m.gl.Lkw. offen."

Below: According to a report in "Die Wehrmacht 1941", this Krupp L 3 H 163 truck loaded with fuel caught fire accidentally in the middle of a Russian village. The driver was able to drive the burning truck to the edge of town and take cover before its cargo exploded.

Upper left: Krupp L 3 H 163 as an anti-aircraft survey troop truck II (Kfz.74): d. long pickaxe, e. oil canister, f. lower mount for winch, g. reserve fuel tank, h. winch, i. off-road chain.

Upper right: A Krupp L 3 H 63 (recognizable by the louvers in the engine hood) as anti-aircraft survey troop truck I (Kfz.74). Crew: Driver and thirteen men. a. off-road chain, b. shovel, c. accumulator. Survey Troop I belonged to Command Post I (survey officer, command device 36), Survey Troop II to Command Post II (battery officer, auxiliary command device 35).

Left: A fully equipped Krupp L 3 H 163 survey truck II (Kfz.74): 1. Reporting device for 4 m R(H) range finder, 2. Em 4 m R(H) (three-dimensional altitude finder), 3. Base for Am 17, n. Telephone throttle case for auxiliary command device, u. Am 17 (range corrector), v. Em 4 m R(H) base, x. Extender, z. Battery 4 Bl. 25 for lights for Em 4 m R(H), a. Battery for command telephone.

Left: Anti-aircraft survey troop truck II (Kfz.74), Krupp L 3 H 163: j. Cable drum with 50 meters of electric cable, k. Apparatus base with three batteries, l. Apparatus, m. Rear handle, n. cable drum with auxiliary telephone cable (60 meters).

Lower left: Rear view of the vehicle shown above (Kfz.74): n. Range finder 4 (R(H), o. Reporting device for range finder, p. Large tent, q. Distributor case, r. Range finder equipment case.

Below: Fuel tank truck (Sd.Kfz.5) on Krupp L 3 H 163 chassis; capacity 3600 liters.

Right: An interesting vehicle of the Nebeltruppen (fog/smoke generating troops), a Krupp L 3 H 163 with double cab. The crew of the leader and six men are unloading the launcher cart of the 10 cm fog launcher. The top bows are carried in front of the cab. (WH 101 232)

Left: At a Flemish railroad crossing in 1940, a Krupp L 3 H 163, clearly showing the towing cable attachment and the individually replaceable radiator elements. In the background is a Krupp L 2 H 143 as Kfz.69, followed by a Ford V8 truck.

Above: Body of an airport spotlight (Siemens-Schuckert) truck, Krupp L 3 H 163. The spotlights could be lifted by scissors jacks.

Left: Airport searchlight truck (Kfz.353) with Krupp L 3 H 163 chassis. Crew: Driver and one attendant.

Krupp Trucks, Commercial Types

The many trucks needed for civilian undertakings were an important part of the German supply system.

Krupp trucks produced in the 1930s:
LD 2 H 42, L 2 H 42, LD 2 H 142, LD 2 H 43, L 2 H 43, L 2 H 143.
LD 2.5 H 42, L 2.5 H 42, LD 2.5 H 142.
LD 3 M 22, L 3 M 22, LD 3 H 62, L 3 H 62, L 3 N 62, L 3 N 63, L 3 H 63, L 3 H 163.
LD 3.5 M 132, L 3.5 M 162, LD 3.5 M 222, L 3.5 M 242.
L 5 M 242.
LD 6.5 N 42, LD 6.5 N 342, L 6.5 N 62.

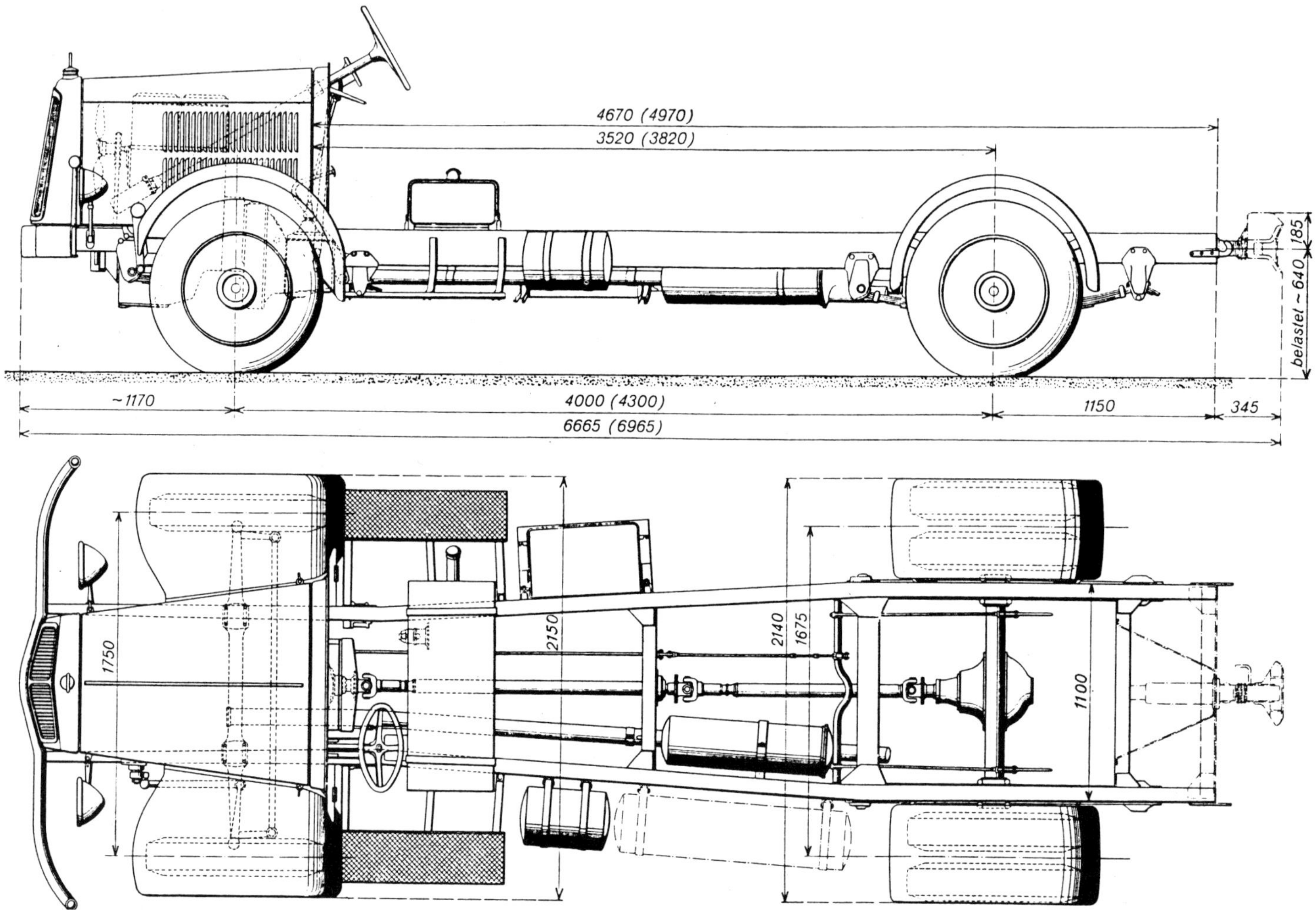

Factory drawing of the Krupp LD 3.5 M 222 (60 HP Diesel engine M402) or Krupp L 3.5 M 242 (75 HP carbureted engine M202).

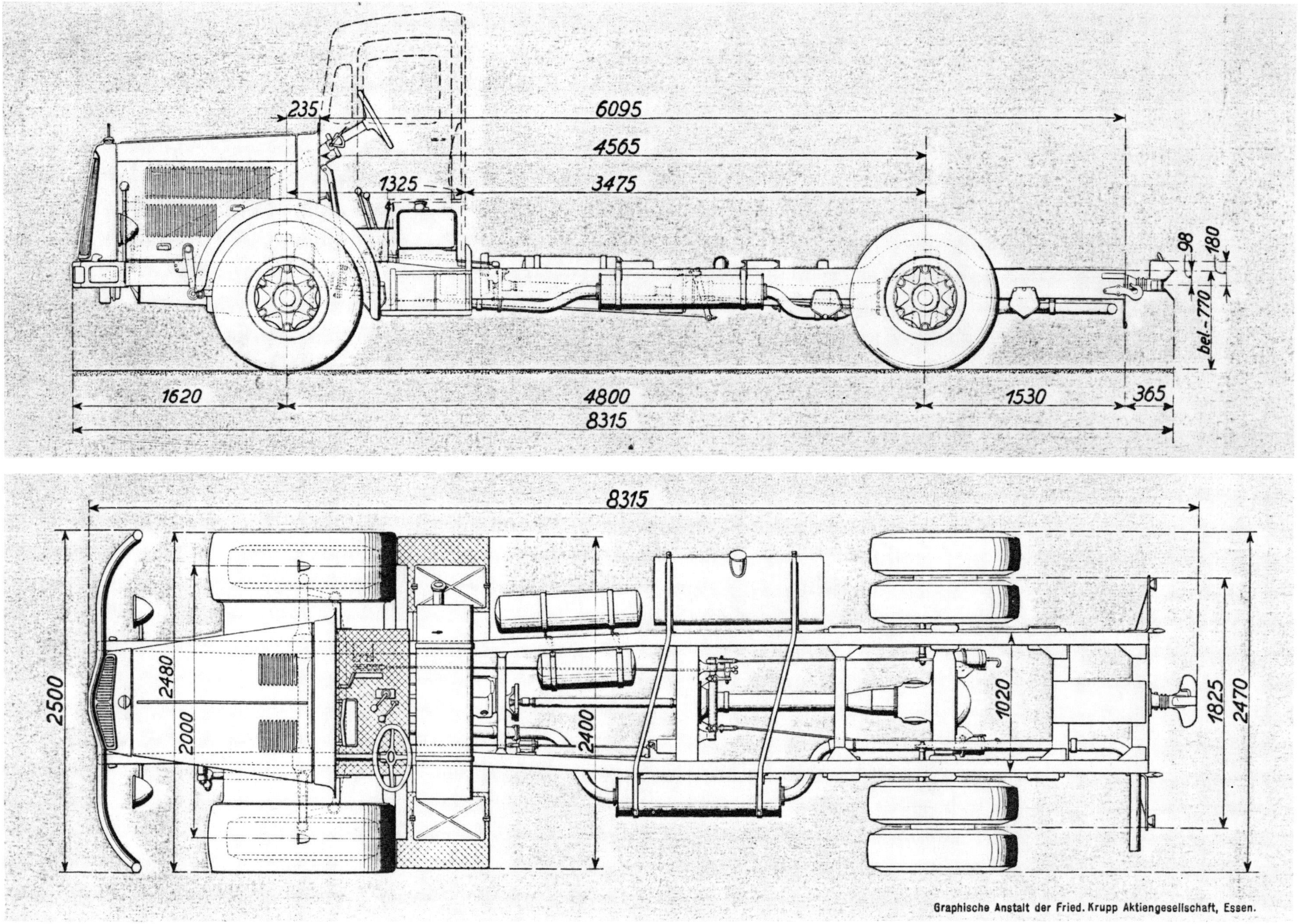

Factory drawing of the Krupp LD 6.5 N 342 with 125 HP M 422 Diesel engine, made under license from Junkers.

Left: The most important Krupp truck used by army long-distance transport units was the 6.5 ton type. This is a Krupp LD 6.5 N 342 with M 422 Diesel engine. In the D 635/5 of July 7, 1943, "Vehicles in Winter", the L 3 H 163 and L 2 H 142 Krupp trucks are described along with the LD 6.5 N 242, forerunner of this type.

Above: A modern-looking 3.5-ton 1940 army truck, the LD 3.5 M 222 with M 402 Diesel engine. This vehicle was identical to the L 3.5 M 242 with M 202 gasoline engine.

Below: Developed for the Wehrmacht but not introduced was the Krupp LD 3 H 62 with M 113 Diesel engine (80 HP). The camouflaged headlights were fitted at the factory.

According to the lettering on the windshield, this Krupp 3.5- or 4-ton truck was used by the OKW on the eastern front. This type is easy to recognize by the bulge on the right side of the hood, caused by the "intake-sound-damper air filter" of the 90 HP M 412 Diesel engine, licensed by Junkers (above).

NSKK members service a 3-ton Krupp truck, either an LD 3 M 22 (M 401 Diesel) or (below) L 3 M 42 (M 202 gasoline engine).

Above: Oxygen tank truck (Kfz.317) on the chassis of the civilian Krupp 5-ton truck with M 12 6-cylinder, 100 HP gasoline engine.

Below: In the 1920s, Krupp built a variety of public service trucks, such as this 3 cubic meter sweeper-flusher on the 5-ton chassis. Many of these trucks were exported, especially to the Soviet Union.

Above: Panzerjäger Unit 44 (1st Mountain Division) had a series of towing trucks with built-in 37mm Pak guns (rebuilt by the troops). Here such an "assault gun" fires across the Marne at Chateau-Thierry on June 12, 1940. Note the pressed-steel frame with the wheel hub lashed to it, the strut on the side and the way the gun wheels are carried. By the short distance between the rear axles, this is a Krupp L 2 H 43.

Below and center: Panzerjäger Unit 44 was loaded at Boom-Antwerp to move "against England" from October 9-14, 1940. Some towing trucks were equipped by the troops with a flat gun stage, strengthened frame, and space for ammunition and baggage at the rear.

Panzerjäger Unit 44 arrives at Celja on the Save in April of 1941. A Krupp L 2 H 43 with fixed 37mm Pak gun and extended shield. Note the high camouflaged headlights and the MP 28/11 on the windshield.

FRIED. KRUPP A.-G.
Essen

KRUPP-DREIACHS-GELÄNDEWAGEN — TYP „L 3 H 163"

MOTOR, GETRIEBE, HINTERACHSE, VORDERACHSE, LENKUNG

Motor: Fabrikat, Typ	Krupp M 12
Zylinderzahl	6, in Reihe
Bohrung	100 mm
Hub	160 mm
Verdichtungsverhältnis	1:5,5
Hubraum	7540 cm³
Gebremste Höchstleistg.	110 PS b. 1600 U/min
Gußform der Zylinder	Block
Ventilanordnung	hängend
Nockenwellenantrieb	Stirnräder, schrägverzahnt
Kurbelwellenlager	7 Gleitlager, das hintere doppelt
Kolbenwerkstoff	Aluminiumlegierung
Ölreiniger	Hirth
Zündung: Art	Magnet
Fabrikat, Typ	Bosch JR 6
Zündfolge	1—5—3—6—2—4
Zündverstellung	von Hand
Anlasser	Bosch BNF 2,5/12 R 9
Lichtmaschine	Bosch RKE 130/12
Batterie	Varta 12 V, 105 Ah
Vergaser	Solex, horizontal
Luftreiniger	Delbag, ölbenetzt
Kraftstofförderung	Membranpumpe
Kühlung	Wasserpumpe
Kupplung	Einscheiben, trocken
Getriebe	ZF-Aphon Gb 45 L mit Zusatzgetriebe
Gangzahl	8 vorw., 2 rückw.
Getriebeuntersetzungen	1:12,5; :6,8; :3,84, :2,23; :4,43; :2,4; :1,35; :0,79; rückw. 1:15,2; :5,35
Höchstgeschwindigkeit	50 km/Std.
Schubübertragung	Schubstangen
Antrieb	Mittel- und H.-Achse
Hinterachsuntersetzung	1:6,33
Vorderachse	Faustachse
Lenkung und Anordnung	Schraube, links
Wendekreisdurchmesser	15,4 m

RAHMEN, FEDERUNG, BREMSEN, RÄDER, MASSE, GEWICHTE

Federn: vorn	Halbfedern längs
hinten	Schraubenfedern
Schmierung	Hochdruckfett, Lub
Vierradbremse: Fabrikat	Knorr
Wirkungsweise	Druckluft
Bremsart der Räder	Innenbacken
Fußbremse wirkt auf	mittlere u. hint. Räder
Handbremse wirkt auf	mittlere u. hint. Räder
Räder: Fabrikat	Hering od. Kronpr.
Art	Stahlblechscheiben
Reifen: vorn	7,25—20 extra
Mitte, hinten	7,25—20 extra ×2
Spurweite: vorn	1740 mm
Spurweite: Mitte, hinten	1729 mm
Radstand:	
Vorder- bis Mittelachse	3650 mm
Mittel- bis Hinterachse	1100 mm
Rahmenoberkante über Boden, vollbelastet	760 mm,
Bodenfreiheit	265 mm, Hinterachse
Gewicht des Fahrgestells	3500—3900 kg
des offenen Aufbaus	1000 kg
Tragfähigk. d. Fahrgest.	3700 kg als Geländefahrzeug, 5700 kg als Straßenfahrzeug
Kraftstoffverbrauch	30 l/100 km
Ölverbrauch	0,8—1 l/100 km
Kurbelrückschlagsicherg.	Abschnappkupplung

FRIED. KRUPP A.-G.,
Essen

KRUPP-DREIACHS-GELÄNDEWAGEN — TYP „L 2 H 43"

MOTOR, GETRIEBE, HINTERACHSE, VORDERACHSE, LENKUNG

Motor: Fabrikat, Typ	Krupp M 304
Zylinderzahl	4, je 2 gegenläufig
Bohrung	90 mm
Hub	130 mm
Verdichtungsverhältnis	1:5,2
Hubraum	3308 cm³
Gebremste Höchstleistg.	60 PS b. 2500 U/min
Gußform der Zylinder	einzeln
Ventilanordnung	hängend
Nockenwellenantrieb	Stirnräder, schrägverzahnt
Kurbelwellenlager	2 Gleitlager
Kolbenwerkstoff	Aluminiumlegierung
Ölreiniger	A. C.
Zündung: Art	Magnetzünder
Fabrikat, Typ	Bosch
Zündfolge	1—3—2—4
Zündverstellung	von Hand, autom.
Anlasser / Lichtmaschine	Siemens-Schuckert-Lichtanlasser LAK 300 K/5
Batterie	Varta 12 V, 75 Ah
Vergaser	Solex BFLH 40, hor.
Luftreiniger	Elektron, ölbenetzt
Kraftstofförderung	Kolbenpumpe
Kühlung	Luft mit Gebläse
Kupplung	Einscheiben, trocken
Getriebe	ZF-Aphon Gb 35 L m. Zusatzgetr. GG 35
Gangzahl	8 vorw., 2 rückw.
Getriebeuntersetzungen	1:12,2; :2,96; :6,37; :2,22; :5,5; :1,59; :3,52; :1; rückw. 1:15,5; :7
Höchstgeschwindigkeit	70 km/Std.
Schubübertragung	Doppelschwingen aus Stahlrohr
Antrieb	Mittel- u. Hinterachse
Hinterachsuntersetzung	1:5,25
Vorderachse	Faustachse
Lenkung und Anordnung	Schnecke, links
Wendekreisdurchmesser	10 m, außen

RAHMEN, FEDERUNG, BREMSEN, RÄDER, MASSE, GEWICHTE

Federn: vorn	Halbfedern längs
hinten	Schraubenfedern
Schmierung	Hochdruckfett, Lub
Sechsradbremse:	
Fabrikat	Ate-Lockheed
Wirkungsw.	Öldruck
Bremsart der Räder	Innenbacken
Bremsart des Getriebes	Außenband
Fußbremse wirkt auf	sechs Räder
Handbremse wirkt auf	Getriebe
Räder: Fabrikat	Hering o. Kronprinz
Art	Stahlblechscheiben
Reifen: vorn, Mitte, hint.	7,50—17 extra
Spurweite: vorn	1580 mm
Mitte, hinten	1555 mm
Radstand:	
Vorder- bis Mittelachse	2470 mm
Mittel- bis Hinterachse	860 mm
Rahmenoberkante über Boden: vollbelastet	640 mm
Bodenfreiheit	255 mm, Mitte und Hinterachse
Gewicht d. Fahrgestells	1700 kg
Tragfähigk. d. Fahrgest.	1800 kg als Geländefahrzeug
Kraftstoffverbrauch	18 l/100 km
Ölverbrauch	0,6 l/100 km
Kurbelrückschlagsicherg.	vorhanden

Also available from Schiffer Military History

OPERATION BARBAROSSA
OSTFRONT 1944
ROMMEL IN THE DESERT
PANZERKORPS GROßDEUTSCHLAND
THE HEAVY FLAK GUNS
THE WAFFEN SS
THE 1st PANZER DIVISION
THE GERMAN INFANTRY HANDBOOK

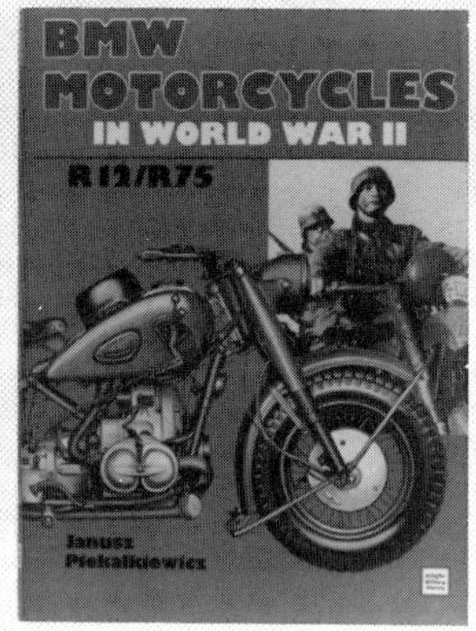